Maria W Jones

A Quaker Love Story

And Other Poems. Second Edition

Maria W Jones

A Quaker Love Story
And Other Poems. Second Edition

ISBN/EAN: 9783744705349

Printed in Europe, USA, Canada, Australia, Japan

Cover: Foto ©Thomas Meinert / pixelio.de

More available books at **www.hansebooks.com**

And so, my dear, thou fain wouldst hear
About my girlhood days.

A

QUAKER LOVE STORY,

AND

OTHER POEMS.

BY

MARIA W. JONES.

SECOND EDITION.

CHICAGO :

M. W. JONES, 76 CALUMET BUILDING.

1885.

Contents.

Note.

The following Quaker Love Story, told first by the heroine nearly sixty years ago, and now retold in verse, has, I fear, little to recommend it but its simplicity and truthfulness; "A certain sweet New Testament plainness"—to borrow one of Charles Lamb's inimitable expressions—having always been a distinguishing characteristic of the Friends.

The greater number of the remaining poems have already appeared in The Scribner, Century, Current, Independent, Christian Union, Weekly Magazine, and other publications of the day.

> "What is writ is writ;
> Would it were worthier."

M. W. J.

CHICAGO, 9th MO., 1885.

Prelude.

The dear old twilight stories
   I heard at mother's knee
Still float, in echoed sweetness,
   Down through the years to me.

And still, as then, seems better
   And dearer than the rest,
A quaint ancestral story—
   One mother loved the best—

Of a sweet Quaker maiden,
   Who, in one far spring day,
Rode off to do God's errand,
   And lost her heart away.

(11)

A QUAKER LOVE STORY

OF THE OLDEN TIME.

1.

AND so my dear, thou fain wouldst hear about my girl-
hood days,
And my long ride with Tacy Gray across rough mountain
ways.
To-day I've thought it over, as I went about my tasks,
And I believe it will be right to grant thee what thou asks.

2.

For it may be a strength to thee, to know how I was led
Through all these years along life's path, and gently shep-
herded.
I have not yet forgotten how, in my earliest youth,
By mother's side in meeting, I felt tenderings of Truth.

13

3.

By the solemn silence quickened, the conscious tear would
    start;
And now and then a trembling sigh, from some contrited
·   heart,
Would rise and beat its viewless wings a moment 'gainst the
    air,
And emphasize the stillness, as an amen does a prayer.

4.

If, when a Friend was moved to speak, the Word with power
    came,
I felt it search my little heart like penetrating flame.
Again, like dew upon the grass, the Spirit's precious dole
Fell on the tender leaves of faith unfolding in my soul.

5.

But yet the world attracted me, and, as I grew in years,
My plain dress was a cross I bore with some rebellious tears.
It seems strange now, in looking back, what weight the out-
    ward had,
And how I tried to compromise betwixt the good and bad.

6.

But compromises only feed the tempted heart's unrest.
A clear renunciation ends the struggle, and is best.
The Lord helped me to see it so, and gave me sweet
    release,
And then, I wore our garb, and yet was clothed upon with
    peace.

7.

I think it was soon after that, when I was twenty-three,
It was borne in on my mind that the Master called for
    me
To go as a companion for our dear friend Tacy Gray
To Virginia Yearly Meeting, and the meetings there
    away.

8.

We started in the spring-time, one early Fifth-month morn,
A dewy freshness filled the air, the world seemed newly
    born,—
The birds like joys embodied went floating in the sheen,
Or sang amid brown twigs outlined in mists of tender
    green.

9.

And I remember now, as if it were but yesterday,
How quickly joyous Nature brushed my farewell tears
    away.
Ah, when we are at peace within, the heart will lightly
    rise
Like a free bird, and earth will seem the long lost paradise.

10.

There were no public coaches went across the mountains
    then—
For this was twenty years ago, in eighteen hundred ten—
And the usual way of travel was by horseback in that
    day,
And even now it seems to me 'tis the ideal way.

11.

I can come so near to nature, for my horse finds all paths
    free;
Between him and his rider is so close a sympathy,
That the sinewy, swift motion which to him belongs
    alone,
Gives me a sense of freest strength as if it were my own.

12.

Just at the last Friend David Gray concluded not to go;
He could not see his way quite clear, but Jabez Shillito—
A kind of inexperienced man—was going part our way,
Whom father thought would be no use, but I heard mother
    say,

13.

"Nay, William! like the effigy thou in thy field didst
    set,
I really think the man will do; for people are not yet
Much wiser than the birds,—we often say: 'There some
    man goes;'
When, after all, the creature owes his sole importance to his
    clothes."

14.

It was a goodly distance—four hundred miles or more—
For two women upon horseback; but the Holy Spirit bore
Us company and comfort, and we never had a fear;
Our greatest dangers are the ones that lurk within, my
    dear.

2

15.

I had never seen the mountains; and now, when from some
 steep,
I saw, e'en to the sky's pale brim, the circling, billowy sweep
Of verdant fields, and forests—now shadowed and now
 bright—
Earth's glory broke upon me in a flood of deep delight.

16.

We stopped at night at any house near which we chanced to
 be,
At wayside inn, or farmer's home, and Tacy, frequently,
Was shown the state of some dear souls which were in bond-
 age led;
And, faithful to the inward voice, she left them comforted.

17.

One evening near our journey's end (we had been ten days
 out),
We queried with a colored man, upon the road, about
Our way.   We hoped to find some Friends residing in that
 part,—
For Friends, though strangers in the flesh, are always friends
 in heart.

18.

"Down dis road hy'ar, aboot a mile, lives Massa Clark," he
said;

"And down dat lane, aboot de same, lives Massa Ben White-
head.

Dey's bof yous kind of people, 'taint no diffaence, I s'pose,

Which way you takes; for heaps of Friends to bof der
houses goes."

19.

We say: "This way or that? It does not matter which we
name."

Lightly we choose, and lo! our lives are nevermore the same!

But they who take the Spirit for their Comforter and Guide

May rest content, for, soon or late, they shall be satisfied.

20.

Tacy a moment waited for the inward "yea" or "nay,"

Then, turning down the lane, she said: "Come, dear, we go
this way."

We found our host a bachelor, with servants quite alone;

Then, I wondered if dear Tacy had indeed been rightly
shown!

21.

Next day we went to Wain Oak, where the Meeting was
to be,
A Friend took Tacy in his gig; our host rode off by me!
And somehow after that, all through the Yearly Meeting
week,
When he spoke to me, 'twas as if, a friend from home did
speak.

22.

It came to pass that Friends arranged when Yearly Meeting
closed,
That he, as he had time and was seriously disposed,
Should attend with us the meetings belonging to our sect,
And visit scattered families as Best Wisdom might direct.

23.

Of course, Benjamin rode mostly along by Tacy's side,
And I, a silent list'ner, was content, and edified
To hear them talk of Early Friends—how clear their call,
and sure,
To come out from the world, and be separate and pure.

24.

And Tacy thought that in our day the call was still the same;
She tenderly admonished us, in the dear Master's name,
To keep ourselves unspotted from the world; take up the
cross
And follow Him, count all men brothers, and Time's glory
dross.

25.

And, dear, I feel to counsel thee, as she did us two then,
To read George Fox's journal through; there thou wilt find
why men
Were once constrained to think the *verily* of Quaker Fox
Was more than the strong oaths of men who haled him to
the stocks.

26.

In stocks, in prison, stoned and scoffed, our Early Friends
stood true;
They spoke the word, they did the deed God gave to them
to do.
And Cromwell said, when he had looked upon George Fox's
face,
" Now is a people risen, not won by gift nor place."

27.

Thus ran our talk, by field and stream, as we went on our
  way,
But lapsing into silence at the far end of the day;
Or, when we entered some pine wood, where each tall, dusky
  tree
Stood like a grave, black cowlèd monk, whisp'ring—Eternity.

28.

Sometimes, when it would happen so that Benjamin would
  ride,
In all the goings to and fro, a brief time at my side,
I was half scared and half ashamed the moment he had gone;
For, like a child which thinks aloud, I feared my tongue ran
  on.

29.

I think though that our thoughts unfold more freely in the
  air,
Where birds and trees, and bloom and bees, their sweets
  together share.
'Tis nature's way! no life with her keeps to itself apart;
And so I shared the thoughts which then kept budding in
  my heart.

30.

Those long rides and the meeting hours were times of deep
content.

The cross I bore when leaving home was gone; but how it
went,

Or why 'twas gone, I neither asked myself nor understood,

I only knew it never seemed so easy to be good.

31.

But, dear, take heed! when our lines fall into a pleasant place,

It is not always safe to think that 'tis God's precious
grace

Within our hearts, which mellows them and makes them
glad and kind;

For, mayhap, we, when trouble comes, our old hard hearts
shall find.

32.

One day at Black Creek Meeting, when Benjamin had led

Our horses up, as usual, for us "to mount," he said,

While looking up at Tacy—it was well he turned from
me—

"I find that I must say farewell, and here part company."

33.

I heard no more—my heart stood still—the earth swam in
    eclipse;
Though when at last he came to me, I said, with steady
    lips,
Some farewell words, then rode away—I would not have
    him know
How, like a ship in sudden storm, my heart reeled to and fro.

34.

But after that, while we remained among Virginia Friends,
I listened as one listens when the hungry heart attends,
For some news dropped of Benjamin, some talk of his
    intent;
But all in vain! I heard no word of why or where he
    went.

35.

The next week Tacy's husband came, and in a few weeks more
We to Ohio all returned, and Tacy truly bore
The sheaves of Peace, but I—I bore a heart of sad unrest,
Though still the Spirit whispered, "The Lord knows what
    is best."

36.

Autumn had come ere we went back. On hill and mountain
    side
Nature had built her altar fires; the trees stood glorified
In unconsuming wondrous flame, like unto sunset dyes,
And morning mists rose up from them as incense to the
    skies.

37.

Yet sadness like a sombre vail lay spread o'er everything,
I thought it was the difference between the Fall and
    Spring;
But, dear, the difference was in me—the vail was on my eyes;
The earth was just as beautiful and just as glad the skies.

38.

" Elizabeth," said father, in the evening after tea—
That first home-coming night when they left mother, him
    ·and me,
To have a little talk alone—"A friend of thine was here—
A friend from Old Virginia, Elizabeth, my dear,—"

39.

Spoke mother, breaking in, for mother had her views
Of what was right in keeping back the best of any news.
"I reckon thou canst guess his name" with slow speech fa-
    ther said.
Then mother spoke right out: "My child, 'twas Benjamin
    Whitehead!"

40.

And once again my heart stood still, then loudly on it went,
I almost thought they'd hear it beat, and wonder what it
    meant.
"He seems a well-concerned young man," said father, talk-
    ing on.
And then I faltered out: "Thou saidst he had been here,
    and gone?"

41.

"Yes," father made reply, "he has gone on about some land."
"William," coaxed mother, reaching out her kind, persua-
    sive hand,
"Thou art too slow!"   "He asked our leave, Elizabeth, my
    dear,
To speak to thee, and child," she said, "Fifth-day he will be
    here."

42.

And so he came, and all was well; my dear, what didst thou
   say?
O yes! he found at Black Creek, in the meeting that last day,
That all his heart was turned to me, but then he could not
   say
One word without my parents' leave; for that he went away.

43.

We handed our intentions into meeting the next spring,
And were married in the Fifth month.   Dear Tacy's offering
Of fervent prayer, when we had said the words that made
   us one,
Fell sweetly on our wedded hearts, like holy benison.

44.

I little thought, when I came home, that I so soon should
   ride
Across those same rough mountain ways, by Benjamin's own
   side.
God's purposes are hid with Him, and silently they grow
Until what perfect time He wills we too shall see and
   know.

45.

Before we went, the way seemed clear for Benjamin to buy
This farm right next to father's, and together he and I
This lofty site chose for our home, and named it Prospect
    Hill;
We thought it then earth's fairest spot, and, dear, we think
    so still.

PROSPECT HILL.

46.

I do not mean there really is no other spot so fair;
But when we sauntered arm in arm, a newly-wedded pair,
Through the long lane up to our farm, in evening's sunset
    glow,
And watched the shadows slowly creep up from the vale
    below,

47.

And saw upon the village hill the sunlit windows shine,
I think no hearts were happier than Benjamin's and mine.
It was the happy inner glow, as well as that without—
That sweet, syllabic sound of "*ours*," I haven't any
    doubt,

48.

Which made it then, and makes it now to us the place most
    fair:
We relatively judge such things, but we must have a care,
In intercourse with others, about the words we use;
For language is a precious gift that suffers much abuse.

49.

There's Benjamin just coming in; I hear him at the door;
I wish that thou wouldst see about—but wait, this one thing
     more
I want to add, while on my mind, for nothing is more sure:
Truth is the salt of character which keeps it sweet and pure.

Other Poems.

MY RICHES.

GRAY as the day, and poor and cold
  Seemed life to me; my tears dropped down,
Blurring from sight the garment old
That lay unpatched the while I told
  My grieving heart how Fortune's frown
Grew darker still.   To others came
Beauty and wealth, dear love and fame;
  But I—I had my torn old gown.

I said—and wept more bitterly—
  I might as well be stricken blind,
If there is naught all day to see
But four bare walls staring at me,
  Blank as my life.   O, fate, unkind!
So prodigal of gifts to some,
Shall gracious beauty never come
  In shape or tint, my home to find?

3

Like a rebuke from God, there came
    A sunbeam to my small, bare room,
And held my gaze in its pure flame
Till rebel thought and fretful blame
    In it seemed slowly to consume.
At peace once more, I raised my eyes,
And saw that in the western skies
    The cold gray day had burst in bloom.

I watched its sunset flower grow
    From matchless bud to matchless rose;
Then saw new glory overflow
And drown the rose in brighter glow
    Of golden light, and still disclose
New loveliness of shape and hue,
Which, ever as I gazed, updrew
    My heart to heights of sweet repose.

Riches and beauty for the world!
    I cried.   Thou unlost Paradise!
Changing from bloom to isles impearled
In golden seas, to flags unfurled

O'er domes and minarets that rise
From jeweled walls, then disappear
Lost, in a fire-fringed sapphire mere,
  Where white and weird a great ship lies.

God surely meant no life should be
  All bare of beauty—wondrous sky!
When, in His love, endowing thee
With richest grace of land and sea,
  He gave thee place to overlie
All life. So mine! I am not poor;
For thy gold falls upon my floor,
  Thy priceless pictures charm my eye.

A VISION.

A LOVELY being, sweet and fair,
   Lips parted, as in blessing,
A bright'ning halo round her hair,
   Hands outstretched for caressing.

And night by night her glad wise eyes
   Foreshine their nearer glory
With glimpse and gleam of Paradise,
   And grand prophetic story.

But morn by morn I wake to find
   The old unlifted sorrow,
And just as far away the kind,
   Dear vision—called To-morrow.

WHAT DOST THOU FEAR?

"The world, the flesh, and the devil."

WHAT dost thou fear, O coward heart,
    That thou dost tremble so?
Though thunderbolts are hurled
    At thee, dost thou not know
That God Himself doth take thy part
    Against a stormy world?

Why long for rest, O weary heart?
    Though care and pain and strife
Hinder and mar the mesh
    Thou weavest of thy life;
Yet God Himself doth take thy part
    Against rebellious flesh.

O, why despair, thou doubting heart?
    God put thee here!   No right
Hast thou to moan—"At length,
    Adversely goes the fight;"
For God Himself doth take thy part
    Against the devil's strength.

ENOUGH.

FROM a cleft in a rock a harebell grew,
    And gathered of rain, and sunshine, and dew,
Its measure of life, in its cup of blue.

In a cabin, out in a western wild,
A maiden bent over her work, and smiled—
For the old, old story her heart beguiled.

The world is wide; but a bit of its earth,
In the cleft of the rock, gave beauty birth
And nourishment meet for its own sweet worth.

The world is wide! but the maiden well knew
No heart in it all was more fond and true
Than the one that her troth was plighted to.

COMMONPLACE.

ONCE I heard a dandelion say—
  Some folks hear, in a curious way,
    Voices mute to others—
"Dandelions are so commonplace,
Without any special gift or grace,
    What's the use of blooming?

" Could I only be a tube rose sweet,
Life indeed would offer something meet
    For my best endeavor.
But a dandelion!   Dear, O dear!
I have yearnings for another sphere
    Not so *very* common."

Hardly had she ceased her mournful plaint,
Hung her head, with grief and chagrin faint,
    When some children spied her,
And in chorus all began to shout:
" The dandelions are coming out;
    The dear dandelions."

Later on, a poet of sweet note
Smiled upon her, and a poem wrote,
    Calling dandelions
The bright gold which Spring, with lavish hand,
Scatters broadcast over all the land
    For dear little people.

"It were better," wrote he, "to forego
All the stately flowers that may blow
    In conservatories
Than that little children should e'er miss
Largess full and golden, such as this—
    Spring time's dandelions."

It were better, thought I, to forego
All the wonders that the *savans* know,
    Than life's lowly duties.
Thus I took the lesson to my heart,
Glad, once more, to do my simple part
    'Mongst the commonplaces.

WAITING.

STEEPED in sunshine, bathed in dew,
Year by year, the strange plant* grew,
But no grace of flower knew.

Seeing it a zealot said,
Hotly shaking his young head,
"Without works one is as dead."

Did it start impatient then,
Try to break its bands of green
With the life which throbbed between?

Nay! it seemed but as before,
Though it may have more and more
Life's sweet pain have pondered o'er.

  *   *   *   *

Many years had come and passed,
And the plant, still bloomless, cast
Broader shadows. But, at last,

---

* The Century Plant.

One fair morning, going by,
Some one looked, and, with a cry,
Called the people far and nigh.

For, from out the circling green
There uprose a wondrous sheen,
Bud and bloom did overlean

The broad leaves, and climb so high,
All their beauty none could spy,
Save the tender, smiling sky.

"'Tis a tree of soft, pale flame,
Greenly whorled," said one who came,
Trying vainly thus to name

Such unwonted loveliness.
In their prodigal excess,
Bud and bloom seemed numberless.

But the zealot humbly said,
Bowing low his hoary head:
" Lo! it teaches in my stead.

" Now I know that soul is great,
Which, aware of its estate,
Nobly is content to wait.

"As for me, O foolish man!
I have learned that no one can
Sit in judgment on God's plan.

" When 'tis time for deed or flower,
He alone can strike the hour
From the heights of His watch-tower."

THE CHERRY FESTIVAL OF HAMBURG.

HARD by the walls of Hamburg town,
 Four centuries ago,
Procopius his soldiers led
 To fight their German foe.
The blue sky bent above the earth
 In benediction mute,
The tranquil fields reposed content
 In blossom, grain, and fruit.

But vain the *"benedicite"*
 Of tender brooding sky,
And vain, the peaceful, smiling fields
 Gave eloquent reply.
Unsoothed! unmoved! in nature's calm,
 The Hussite army lay,
A threat'ning, deadly, *human* storm,
 With Hamburg in its way.

To swift destruction now seemed doomed
  The dear old German town.
Before Procopius the Great
  The strongest walls went down.
But, hark! what means this muffled sound
  Of swift advancing feet?
Was Hamburg ready after all
  Its hated foe to meet?

The Hussites quickly sprang to arms!
  The great gate opened wide;
And out there poured, not armèd men,
  But, marching side by side,
Came little children of the town,
  Whose round eyes met their gaze
With innocence that courage was
  Unlearned in worldly ways.

The men threw all their weapons down
  At sight so strange and fair!
They took the children in their arms,
  They smoothed their flaxen hair;

They kissed their cheeks and sweet red lips,
　　They told how, back at home,
They left such little ones as they,
　　And then they bade them come

To cherry orchards, close at hand,
　　And there they stripped the trees
Of branches rich with clustered fruit.
　　Their little arms with these
They filled, and with kind words of peace,
　　They sent them back to town,
And all the soldiers marched away,
　　Nor thought of their renown.

And now, each year in cherry time
　　In Hamburg, one may see
The little children celebrate
　　This strange sweet victory.
Again the tramp of little feet
　　Is heard, as side by side
They march all through the quaint old town
　　In childhood's joyous pride.

Again, within their arms they bear
  Green branches, through whose leaves
Ripe cherries gleam, and tell a tale
  More strange than fancy weaves,
About a bloodless battle fought
  Four hundred years ago,
When children saved old Hamburg town
  By conquering its foe.

CARRIE

A WINSOME little girl,
  As pure as milk-white pearl,

As sweet as fragrant rose,
As blithe as bird that knows

Only to soar and sing,
On swift ecstatic wing.

So glad of life—of love—
Of sunny sky above,

Of all these things, so glad!
Can she be ever sad?

Ah, yes! so sad is she
O'er broken wing of bee,

O'er homeless dog or cat,
Or any creature that

God made and man forgets
To care for, that she sets

Me wondering how He,
More pitiful than she,

Endures so patiently
Man's inhumanity.

FOR OTHERS' SAKE.

"Live pure, speak true, right wrong, follow The Christ—else
wherefore born?"—*Idyls of the King.*

A ROUND King Arthur's table came
    Brave, stalwart men, who, soon or late,
Won for themselves a famous name,
    And climbed up to a knight's estate.
And each one sought some maiden's smile,
    Her "favor" on his helmet wore,
On deeds of errantry—the while
    She praised and loved him more and more.

And poet's idyls, new and old,
    Cease not to tell the wondrous tale,
How these good knights, so true and bold,
    Rode forth to make some tyrant quail
In his stronghold; for ladies fair
    Risked life and limb, and thought no deed
Too hard for them to do or dare,
    Could they but win the hero's meed.

O, grand the story of brave deed,
   And sweet the guerdon bravely won;
So brave, so sweet, that as we read,
   Electric currents swiftly run
From noble lives of ages past,
   And thrill our hearts, until we fain
Would live as they, as they at last,
   Such love, such praise, such honor gain.

Nor are there wanting men of might,
   Nor wrongs to tilt a free lance for;
Nor now need maidens, out of sight,
   Wait weeping till the battle's o'er.
Some cycles nearer has earth rolled
   To the eternities, whose light
On it more broadly falls.   Behold!
   God's truths shine out in clearer sight.

And now has gentle woman found
   To *do* is finer than to *be*,
That our King at whose "Table Round"
   There sitteth " neither bond nor free,

Nor male nor female "—He doth make
  Us " one in Him "—gives unto all
Something to do for others' sake,
  Some blows to strike for error's fall.

For other's sake, O men of might!
  For other's sake, O women fair!
Spurn from your taste, your touch, your sight,
  Circean draughts which hide a snare
That robs the nation of its men,
  Wives of their husbands and their sons;
Yea, God of His earth-born, and them
  Of heaven and its shining ones.

For others' sake! O strong! O sweet!
  O common tie! that binds our way
To God's great throne, when we repeat
  In such small measure as we may,
The earth-life of His own dear Son,
  Who lived and died for others' sake—
For others' sake God's heaven won
  By cross and curse none else could take.

KING WATER.

O WONDROUS! beyond all compare,
  Is the palace spacious and fair
And high as the infinite air—
    Of water, the king.
Its walls and its roof are the skies,
Whose far deep'ning glory outlies
The uttermost reach of our eyes,
    Or bird's swiftest wing.

The king calls the aid of the sun,
And beautiful rainbows are spun,
Which hang a few moments when done,
    Upon his gray walls—
Then fade from our vision away
Like dreams of the night, when the day
From wonderland, changeful and gay,
    The spirit recalls.

Anon he flings over the sun
Such curtains of mist that not one
Tiny ray can creep through, and run
    To earth with its light.
Fiery flames, too, own his command,
They leap up! but cannot withstand
The weight of his cool, mighty hand—
    They sink out of sight.

The earth with its harvests is crowned,
The great wheels of labor go round,
The mills' golden grain heaps are ground
    By help from his throne.
The traveler is sped on his quest
By a steed that needeth no rest;
For this king hath breathed in his breast
    The life of his own.

His voice in the cataract's roar,
In the waves that break on the shore,
Proclaims in our ears evermore
    His glorious might.

And, again, in the musical flow
Of the brook, 'tis silv'ry and low
As the laugh of a child when we know
    It laughs with delight.

But another has set up his throne
In the land this king calls his own,
And by deeds dark and evil has grown
    King Alcohol's fame.
He makes of earth's fruit and its grain
A poison that maddens the brain—
His subjects seek honor in vain.
    They only find shame.

But lo! he now trembles, afraid
Of the nations whose trust he's betrayed,
Whose homes he has desolate made—
    And fain would he bring
Peace off'rings of money—but no!
A voice like the cataracts flow
Shall thunder: "The tyrant must go,
    For Water is King."

BEYOND THE HILLS.

"I WISH that I could go away," sighed Claire,
  Leaning a pensive face upon her hand,
And looking off with wistful eyes, where fair
And far, the hills shut in the quiet land
Whereon her gaze had fallen every day
Since her young life began. "I've half a mind,"
She said, "that I will start and run away—
Like boys do in the story books—and find
What lies beyond those far-off watchful hills."

"I almost feel that I am rooted here
As are the trees within our door-yard small.
They can do naught but stand there year by year,
Until at last they, gnarled and bent, shall fall
As I shall some day on my wrinkled face—
Still looking toward the hills, and old and gaunt,
Still standing in the same familiar place.

I cannot bear it, mother dear, I want
To go—I must go—off beyond the hills."

"And do the trees indeed stand still, my dear?"
Queried the patient mother. "Do they not grow
A little nearer the blue sky each year?
Do not their spreading branches ever throw
A little broader shadow in the sun,
To shelter man and insect, bird and beast?
Of all the gracious leafy trees, which one
Has not a better thought, for you at least,
Than wayward flight beyond the untried hills?"

"Well, I have heard," said Claire, with a slow smile,
Still gazing at the hills, "that there will come
In time—whether one waits upon an isle
Amid the ocean waves or sits at home—
The thing that one above all else desires.
The heart is its own oracle of fate,
The inborn need its prophecy inspires,
And mine to me has whispered, 'Soon or late,
Thou shalt go forth beyond the circling hills.'"

*   *   *   *   *   *

Not late, but soon!   O grievous, dread surprise,
When sobbing friends beheld sweet Claire depart:
Not as she oft had dreamed, but with her eyes
Fast closed in death.   Upon her pulseless heart
And smiling lips, death's solemn secret seal.
"She never had her wish," grieved they with tears,
"How strange it seems that the dear Lord should deal
So sternly with the child.   In all these years
She longed in vain to go beyond the hills."

"She *has* her wish," the gray-haired pastor said,
"She has gone forth beyond the barring hills,
Not with slow feet, a beaten path to tread;
But with swift wings to bear her where she wills.
What matters it if life's periphery
Be small or great?   What traveler now so wise
As this young girl, who sees eternity—
Sees God Himself with her clear angel eyes!
While we are still environed by the hills."

LOVE.

WE'VE all had our lovers; some constant, some not—
  Though each vowed to us everlasting affection—
Some left us in anger; some only forgot,
  And some were dispatched by a simple rejection.

But these people—Ah these! love on without end,
  Regardless of failings of flesh or of temper,
More constant than lover, more loving than friend,
Though all others fail, they are *fideles semper*.

They pour out their love for our commonest use,
  Unmindful of circumstance, care, or requiting;
If smitten on one cheek, they condone the abuse,
  And turn us the other for kissing or smiting.

Ah! when was a lover's love ever like this?
  Enduring all things, still hoping, believing.
Depending on neither a smile nor a kiss,
  Lavish in giving, e'en if little receiving.

No others—not even ourselves—with such zest
    Hear sounded our praises, nor think us so clever;
They hold as better than other folks best—
    God bless these dear fathers and mothers forever!

IN EMBRYO.

TO F. B.

WHAT was life to the moth in its chrysalid thrall?
　　Did it wake 'twixt its dreamings and ask: "Is this all"?
Did it thrill to the tips of its embryo wings
With an impulse for flight born of bright visionings
Flashing by in the wildering maze of a dream,
Then lost as the cloud loses the lightning's swift gleam?

Did the light filter through its soft, silken cocoon
And strike its closed eyes with a vague sense of that boon—
The power of sight?　Did the ambient air break
Softly in waves o'er its walls and bid it awake
And pierce through the strange silence and darkness around
To a beautiful world full of sunlight and sound?
Did it struggle against its invisible chain
Till it grew almost mad with the longing and pain?

I know not. But I know that a hand, never seen,
Cut its bonds all away with strokes subtle and keen,
And one day it came forth from its close prison cell,
Free! strong-winged and clear-eyed! Thus at last it befell
That the great sunlit world, which had once seemed so strange,
This rejoicing, freed creature had now for its range.

     *   *   *   *   *   *

My dear friend, dost thou guess what my thought is for thee?
Does the strain of thy soul reveal captivity?
Dost thou know thy own self, in relation to life,
As only a something with a something at strife?
Does the silence but echo thy wild questionings?
The Divine life within thee is stirring its wings.

Abide! Thy strong soul grows large for its shell,
And some glad blessed day, the same bliss which befell
The beautiful moth shall happen to thee,
And thou, too, shalt know what it is to be free;
What sight is, what life is, and heaven—yea, more—
When thy wings vail thy face as thou bowest before
The Creator of life, life's Redeemer and Guide,
Thou shalt know what it is to be aye satisfied.

EDITH.

7th mo. 3, 1880.

ONLY a year since she entered
  Our goodly and beautiful land,
Where at once she set up her kingdom,
  At once began her command.

With smiles and tears she has conquered;
  Her royal will knows no excuse;
She has no reason for doubting
  That the world was made for her use.

She snares us all by her dimples;
  She enchants us all by her eyes;
She seemeth a pure white lily
  Sweetly blooming in human guise.

Whatever is good and lovely,
  Whatever is dainty and bright,
Appears to her little Highness
  Her own indisputable right.

No gem so rare, nor so costly
  That she would not quietly take
As part of her great possessions,
  And of it——a plaything make.

I saw her look at Niagara
  With a cool, indifferent air,
As if she had seen falls grander,
  And didn't for these much care.

Wonderful things she's been used to!
  That is evident every day;
And nothing so much surprises
  Her as not to have her own way.

Dear little lily-like princess!
  Her strength in her helplessness lies.
She captures our worldly wisdom
  By her looks so unworldly wise.

O may she rule long and sweetly;
  Have happy returns of the day,
And find that they who best govern
  Are they who first learn to obey.

IN MEMORIAM.

DIED—Suddenly, Sabbath evening, April 20, 1879,
Miss Jennie Roberts.

DID a strange, sweet exaltation thrill
　　Her soul that fair last day, as she drew
So near to heaven?　Albeit, still
　　Unconscious, it was opening to her view.

Did the light within, inform her eyes?
　　That she turned so oft to say
To friends—farther off from Paradise—
　　"This is such a lovely, lovely day."

That light, strange and tender, which has place
　　In souls, but was ne'er on sea nor land,
Faded with the eve a little space,
　　Then to heaven brightened as Christ's hand

Led her from death's valley, cold and dim,
　　And before the Father on His throne

Her confessed who erst had confessed Him
   In the fleeting earth-life she had known.

So she passed!   A soul as sweet and shy
   As a violet which, unaware,
Tells to every one who goeth by
   That a fragrant life is blooming there.

Does the violet, when gathered, miss
   The twin flower blooming by her side?
For God's *human* flowers, He reserves the bliss
   Of again together blooming glorified.

O, bereaved ones! if true love alway
   Seeks the happiness of the beloved—
Of its own unmindful—ye can say,
   With a strong affection deeply proved,

And the strength that trusting faith imparts,
   "Heaven is hers!   We but count her gain!"
Folding close within your wounded hearts
   Thoughts of her sweet peace, to heal them of
       their pain.

THE MESSAGE OF THE SNOW.

THE spring with sun, soft airs and rain
  Had wrought its miracles and gone;
Summer and fall, in long, bright train
Of bloom and fruit and waving grain,
Had passed, and sweeter treasures borne.
"Is life," I moaned, "a fateful breath
Forever drawn away by death?
Is there no joy lives on and on?

"The trees grieve over branches bare,
And stretch them up with sobbing cry,
But all in vain is moan or prayer,
I only seem to hear or care,
And helpless watch the leaden sky
And hopeless think of other prayers—
Then wonder if indeed God cares,
Or—if—He's there, to make reply."

Lo! while I wonder, the gray gloom,
Which typified my heart's despair,

Breaks softly into starry bloom
So pure, nor tint, nor faint perfume
Stains these white blossoms of the air,
Which spread, in prodigal excess
Of nature's need, their loveliness
Upon the earth.   The branches bare

That shivered erst in wintry air,
No longer mourn their lush green leaves,
And purer are the robes they wear
Than fuller makes with utmost care,
And softer far than weaver weaves.
The humblest shrub, or meanest thing
Now stands in white apparelling,
And speaks—God's priest—to her who grieves.

" O, troubled heart!   Now wilt thou dare
To longer hopeless mourn?   Behold, .
What wondrous beauty budding where
To thee was only empty air.
Thou knowest naught!   Joys manifold
Shall bloom from out thy sorrow's night
Changing its darkness into light,
For know dear heart, that God *is* there."

CUI BONO?

" I 'M disappointed, tired of life,
    If this be all—to eat, to sleep, to rise
And go about the same dull round
    Of graceless tasks—to ask with sighs
What means this riddle we call life?
    Perpetuated for what end?
Its days like drops of water run
    In tedious, ceaseless repetend.

"Nothing I do seems worth the while,
    As well the world without my deeds,
Since every one can do the same
    .They are as commonplace as weeds.
Insipid is the cup I drink,
    And hateful is my common fate;
My soul immortal fain would read
    The mysteries that palpitate

" Upon the winds, upon the waves,
    And in the bosom of the sky;
From longing soul and universe,
    Deep calls to deep, with endless cry.
Wherefore that cry?   O, wherefore life?
    Strange gift! which none can tell about
Until the breath of unseen death
    Shall blow the feeble taper out."

Thus spoke the girl, impatient grown
    With self—with hard, dull circumstance
That hedged her in from paths up which
    Her restless feet would fain advance.
Her heart was sick with hope deferred,
    With purposes all unfulfilled.
In the world's work-shop of great deeds
    There seemed no place for her to build.

Sighing, she turned to her loved books,
    As daily she was wont to do,
In them to drown accusing thoughts
    Which held her empty life in view.

Half unaware, her wand'ring hand
  Was stayed upon a volume old,
Whose truths unto her holden eyes
  Had been no more than fables told.

But now God's Spirit in her soul
  To her remembrance once more brought
The old, old story, read so oft,
  And henceforth with new meaning fraught.
" My child," He said, " from heaven once,
  The King's own son came down to earth
And lived earth's life of petty toil,
  And set His royal seal of worth

"On smallest deed or simplest task
  For love or homely duty done.
And now shouldst thou but give a cup
  Of water to a thirsty one;
Or, even take a little child
  Up in thy arms and win its smile,
Thou still wouldst do a kingly thing,
  The thing that Christ thought worth His while.

" He helped the hungry, erring, sad,
    And daily taught—not how to solve
Some problem fine, of how the stars
    Around some central sun revolve.
But how each one hath sacred part
    In life's great common brotherhood;
And they live best, who, like God's Christ
    Find their life's use in doing good."

TO A FRIEND.

MARRIED IN APRIL.

O APRIL! month of miracles,
　　What wonders dost thou bring to pass!
Leaves burgeon on the naked trees,
　　Brown fields grow green with tender grass,
Sweet violets, all purple clad,
　　Steal gently forth and, one by one,
Their hoods throw back from faces glad
　　To meet the kisses of the sun.

But sweeter miracle than these,
　　O, month of violets! is wrought
Within the garden of the heart,
　　Where suddenly love comes unsought,
And makes of life a summer day—
　　Though April winds blow cold and chill—
For true love blooms for aye and aye,
　　And will not fade as violets will.

LINES WRITTEN ON BIRCH BARK TO A FRIEND.

FROM a dryad of the wood
  Stolen was this tablet fine,
'Twas her stylus that engraved
  Clearly each unfading line.

Scarcely do I dare to write,
  In my clumsy, human way,
These few words, lest I efface
  Tale or poem of some fay.

But between my written lines
  Thou, with clearer eyes, may'st see
Characters and occult signs
  Untranslatable by me.

Thou may'st read what the wild wind—
  Rover from all lands and seas—

Whispered when he told his love
  To the palpitating trees.

Thou may'st find the mysteries ·
  Revealed here, of all the wood,
Happy secrets of the birds,
  Bees, and streamlets, understood

And interpreted by none,
  Save the fairies and the heart
That the world hath never won,
  Which must needs go oft apart

From the busy haunts of men,
  To the woods and fields to find
Respite, from the "madding crowd"
  Healing, for its wounds unkind.

Sonnets.

PARADISE REGAINED.

THE circling hills of woods and clouds snow-white
Held, in the golden hour of eventide,
The lake by which I walked, and seemed to hide
From view a world yet lovelier, whose light
Streamed up behind their heights and made them glow,
As wrapped in purest flame, and flung on high
Bright flakes of glory 'gainst the pale blue sky,
Which bridged with paths of fire the lake below.
I felt sweet music that I could not hear,
I saw a poem that I could not read,
"What place is this?" I cried! Lo, at my need
Two lovers passed—'twas Paradise! for clear
I saw it shining in his happy eyes,
I heard it murmured in her low replies.

ONWARD TO THE SEA.

ON that broad stream, which bears upon its breast
A thousand isles, we sailed one summer day,
And gazing forward, we were quick to say,
"The green shores meet beyond and must arrest
Our progress." Lo! while yet our lips confest
Our fears, our good ship neared and found a way
Between the isles,—a track that darkling lay
Safe and secure, to speed us on our quest.
Some parted links in every barring chain
We found alway—and sailing on and on,
We came at last into the open main;
As birds on wing, all ways were ours—for, gone
Was every limit, save the circling sky
Which still encompassed as the days went by.

II.

Sailor upon life's stream! dost thou descry
Before thy way high rocks which seem to rise
To thrust thee back? Trust not thy holden eyes,
They cannot see! events shall by and by
Their poor, short-sighted evidence deny:
Give not thy heart to fears, thy lips to sighs,

Nor falter back, and thou, in glad surprise,
Shalt find ere long how God hath made reply
Unto thy need, while yet thou couldst not see;
Between the shores thy pathway lies secure,
The stream flows onward to Eternity
And fain shall carry thee into that pure,
Broad ocean which God's love enspheres—a sky—
Alway encompassing as time goes by.

WEDDING-DAY.

A FRIEND'S IN ENGLAND.

A RAINY April day! with fitful gleams
Of sun, and fitful flight, from dripping eaves,
Of chirping birds to trees whose tender leaves
Scarce lovelier than summer's bloom we deem;
So fair to winter-weary eyes they seem.
But by that necromancy which retrieves
The past, or future happiness perceives,
I conquer time and space, as in a dream,
And see no longer this wet April day;
But one more fair, born under England's skies,
And nearer by a fortnight to sweet May.
But fair or dark, or in whatever guise
It comes—within two hearts it is a day
More bright than any out of Paradise.

April 14, 1882.

TO M. H. P.

MISSIONARY TO CHINA.

TO mine own understanding did I lean
　When—having thee in mind—I said, one day
'Twould be like death to go so far away
That the whole earth would interpose, between
My home and me, its dense opacity.
It would be death—not life—so far apart
From all that feeds and satisfies the heart.
So spake I: but, years later, seeing thee,
I saw I had but uttered half a truth.
Thy face revealed the rest—" Whoso shall lose
His life for Christ's dear sake, *the same in sooth
Shall find it.*"　Some death pangs—then God renews
The life!　Thy happy eyes the secret told
Of blessed gain—not loss—an hundred fold.

TO A PANSY.

"Pansy--that's for thoughts."

THOU lovely thought of God! perfect and fair,
    Unflawed by sin! I cannot e'er repeat
Thy tender meanings, thou dear paraclete;
Be thou my messenger to-day, and bear
Unto my friend—with whom I fain would share
All good and pleasant thoughts—thy beauty sweet,
Through which I feel, like unseen pulses, beat
God's love and power. Then, wilt thou declare.
In gentle breathings to my absent friend,
My love, solicitude, and blessings more
Than I can think or ask for? Let these blend
With heaven's message, thou didst bear before;
And so the deepest feelings of my heart—
For which there are no words—shalt thou impart.

www.ingramcontent.com/pod-product-compliance
Lightning Source LLC
Chambersburg PA
CBHW021522270326
41930CB00008B/1049